REFLECTIONS OF A SOUTHERN BOY

DEVOTIONS FROM THE DEEP SOUTH

JACK CUNNINGHAM

Reflections of a Southern Boy

ISBN: **978-1-7322488-0-9**

Ashland Park Books
Montgomery, Alabama

Cover Design: Teddi Black
Interior Design: Megan McCullough

Author's Note

Portions of this Work have been previously published in periodicals and other publications. The Work, in whole, has not been previously published and is not in the public domain. All Scripture references are taken from the King James Version.

DEDICATION

To my late college pastor Joe Fowler and his wife Wrae,
who first taught me the fundamentals of God's grace.
I am forever grateful.

ACKNOWLEDGMENTS

Thank you, Dr. Dennis E. Hensley, for your advice during the writing of this book. You have been a great encourager and a wise teacher throughout my writing career.

Table of Contents

REFLECTIONS
ON HOLINESS

Don't Flirt

Genesis 13:1-13

And Lot lifted up his eyes and beheld all the plain of Jordan, that it was well watered everywhere, before the LORD destroyed Sodom and Gomorrah, even as the garden of the LORD, like the land of Egypt, as thou comest unto Zoar. Then Lot chose him all the plain of Jordan; and Lot journeyed east; and they separated themselves the one from the other (Genesis 13:10-11, KJV).

One thing about the American South, it sure has lots of good farmland. Corn, cotton, peanuts, and sugar cane are just a few crops grown down my way. Lot, Abraham's nephew, would have liked our lush acreage, I'm sure.

Why? Because when he surveyed the lush Jordan Plain, a long strip of land dotted by rain-filled wadis and streaked by rolling rivers, he imagined it as the perfect place for keeping his livestock watered and fed.

Ah! Now here's the catch. He didn't just choose it for his livestock. Another factor influenced his decision—Egypt. It reminded him of Egypt. Ever since he and his uncle left Ur of the Chaldees, their wealth accumulated to the point where they wallowed in it. Because of their barely manageable possessions, they could no longer travel together. Not only was the land unable to support them, their herdsmen fought each other. This quarrelling, they knew, needed to end.

"All right, Nephew," Abraham said, gesturing at the land around them. "I'll give you a choice. You can go either left or right. And whichever direction you choose, I'll go in the opposite direction."[1]

"I'll go to the right, Uncle," Lot said. He proceeded eastward and pitched his tent near Sodom, in the Valley, the best part of the land.

Everything pleased Lot's eyes, yet evil rampaged throughout Sodom. Despite this, he later packed up and moved his family into that den of sin. To put it bluntly, he compromised. Had the angels of the Lord not rescued him, he might have perished in its squalor.

Lot's experience teaches us an important lesson: don't flirt with sin, nor even go near it. Sure, it may appear attractive on the outside, all shiny and full of fun, like a brand new pickup truck or a freshly painted barn where folks inside are having a lively hoedown. Not that pickups and hoedowns are sinful, because they aren't. Personally, this Alabama boy likes pickups and square dancing. But sin masquerades as similar pleasures. It waves its hand and beckons us, "Come on in! Enjoy yourself."

If we yield to that pseudo-friendly hand, it'll snatch us and ultimately destroy us. Its pleasures are but for a season.[2] One day we'll enter eternity, and those sinful things we thought were fun will be our eternal ruin.

God gives us a choice. We can, like Abraham, either follow Him in faith and fruitfulness; or we can follow Lot's disastrous example. The question is, which direction will we

---

1   Genesis 13:8
2   Hebrews 11:25

go, toward God or toward the world? I don't know about you, but I want to move toward God.

PRAYER: Dear Lord, I want to walk toward You, to be close to You, to draw strength from You, that I might resist temptation. Thank You for this strength, Lord, the power of Your Holy Spirit's enabling working in and through my life. In Jesus' name. Amen.

Brief Reflection

Satan knows our weaknesses and always tempts us at our most vulnerable spots. How can we resist temptation?

Passages for Study

Mark 14:32-42
James 4:4-10
Genesis 39:6-15/ 2 Timothy 2:22-26

Study Notes

My Grandfather's Influence

1 Corinthians 4:14-21

> *For though ye have ten thousand instructors in Christ, yet have ye not many fathers: for in Christ Jesus I have begotten you through the gospel. Wherefore I beseech you, be ye followers of me (1 Corinthians 4:15-16, KJV).*

My mother grew up in a small Alabama town called Brundidge. Many a time during our childhoods, my sister and I journeyed there with our parents. Sitting in our car's backseat, we watched the pastoral landscapes as we rumbled along narrow country roads. Corn and cotton carpeted numerous acres. Cattle grazed other fields. To alleviate our sibling boredom and to keep us reasonably quiet, our parents invented a "counting cows" game. Whoever counted the most cows on their side of the car, till we reached Brundidge, won it.

I don't know about my sister, but I enjoyed this game. And since I was born and reared in big-city Mobile, rural living fascinated me. No beeping cars, no sirens, no busy shopping centers as in my hometown. Just fresh air and peaceful neighbors. Also, my grandparents.

My grandfather's gas station and Ford dealership stood on its main street. Oh, my mind forms wonderful images of my grandparents and this town! The memory that moves front and center, though? My grandfather's walk with God. Little did he realize the impression he'd made on my young mind.

When we prepared for bed I always slept in my grandparents' room. My bed stood against the wall opposite theirs. While snuggled under my sheets, my eyes followed my grandfather's movements. He'd sit in his rocker near a floor lamp, its bulb shining through its opaque shade.

His Bible in his lap, he read God's Word. After a period of time, he closed the Book then knelt beside his bed. His mumbles drifted to my ears, and I knew he was talking with God.

Decades have passed; my grandfather's influence remains. He inspired me to read my Bible and to know God. He never preached with his mouth. His life was a sermon. I'm sure he'd agree with the Apostle Paul, that he would be happy I'm trying to imitate his walk of faith. Thanks to his example, he preserved his grandson from the pain of sin.

PRAYER: Dear Lord, may my life be a sermon of holiness, set apart for Your Kingdom and glory. In Jesus' name. Amen.

Brief Reflection

Because we're all role models to certain people, we model either good behavior or bad. Jesus modeled perfect behavior. Although we'll never be perfect like our Savior, our goal as disciples is to grow into mature, holy sons and daughters. Name one mark of spiritual maturity.

Passages for Study

Matthew 5:43-48
John 13:31-35
Romans 12:1-2

Study Notes

The Funny Farm

Philippians 3:12-21

> *For our conversation is in heaven; from whence also we also look for the Saviour, the Lord Jesus Christ:* (Philippians 3:20, *KJV*).

When I disembarked my plane at Kona International Airport on Hawaii's "Big Island," bearing its state's name, I stood awed. I imagined Captain Cook's sailors perched in their ships' rigging when they first spotted this archipelago's tropical paradise. "Land ho!" I heard them yell.

Did those sailors share my thoughts? What was this island like? My uncle, who'd been here during World War Two, described it to me. Once my explorer's curiosity kicked in, I wanted to discover it for myself.

Wait. I didn't come here for summer vacation. Serious business awaited me during this summer break. I hurried toward the terminal, toward the waves and smiles of those welcoming my arrival. Here I joined youth from other states. We'd come to share the gospel. One day later, after splitting into groups and being dispatched to various towns and districts, we worked under spiritually mature leaders.

A bus carried my group to Hilo, a city on the Big Island's east coast.

On one particular day a California friend and I happened upon a schoolyard where we noticed a little girl playing on a swing by herself.

"Let's go talk to her," my friend Laura said.

We went to the girl, spoke to her, and sat on the grass beside her. I opened my mouth and started to share Christ.

The girl glanced at Laura. "Is he from the funny farm?" Her expression quizzical, the girl knitted her brows. She pointed at me.

"No." Laura touched her tiny hand. "We're Christians."

Again, I started to speak. Brow crinkling, the girl's puzzled gaze fastened on Laura. "He talks funny. Are you sure he's not from the funny farm?"

"No, no. He's fine."

Unconvinced, the girl averted my eyes.

This "funny farm" business continued for another five minutes or so, till Laura finally said, "They all talk that way where he's from."

Gee. Thanks. I chuckled to myself, realizing that I was probably the first Deep South Southerner this little Hawaiian girl had ever met. My accent, my drawl, identified my cultural roots.

When Paul told the Philippians that our conversation is in heaven he wasn't talking about literal speech, but citizenship.

However, if we're citizens of heaven, our literal conversation should set us apart from those who don't yet know Christ. Just as my accent marked me as an American Southerner, so our spiritual accent should let the world know we're Christians. How we talk and how we behave as God's earthly colony should demonstrate our heavenly roots.

By letting our walk line up with our talk, we can spread His good news to others and lead them into heavenly citizenship.

PRAYER: Dear Lord, I want to be a good citizen of my eternal home. By the power of Your Holy Spirit, enable me to live a consistent, holy life. May my walk and my talk represent Your kingdom in a way that pleases You. In Jesus' name. Amen.

Brief Reflection

Hypocrites feign holiness. In their pride and rebellion, they oppose God's standards in their private lives. What did Jesus say about hypocrites?

Passages for Study

Matthew 23:13-36

Study Notes

Odor or Aroma?

2 Corinthians 2:14-17

> *Now thanks be unto God, which always causeth us to triumph in Christ, and maketh manifest the savour of his knowledge by us in every place* (2 Corinthians 2:14, KJV).

During my college years, because I often arrived at church earlier than everyone else, my pastor gave me the key to open up before meetings. On one frigid winter night I rushed to its gas heater, struck a match, lighted it...*swoosh*...flames shot out. I turned it down fast.

Seconds later my pastor and his wife barged through the glass doors.

"Jack! Jack! Your hair's on fire!" my pastor's wife cried, jumping on me and snuffing it out.

Once our meeting started a boy sitting beside me turned to his father. "Hey, Dad, I smell smoke."

His father smiled.

Embarrassment stifled my tongue. I was the one emitting that odor, all right, and I had a feeling his father knew that. Now, many years later, I'm willing to admit I should've known how to light a gas heater. After all, my parents' house had one just like my church's. Since my family used it all the time during winter, I'd lit one before.

So how do we smell? Spiritually, that is. Do we reek of hell's smoke and its odor? Or do we have an aromatic savour; that is, the fragrance of the Holy Spirit that permeates those who follow Christ, who rely on Him to enable them to walk victoriously? When we pour out our lives to Him as a living sacrifice through total surrender to His will, His sweet aroma spreads everywhere we walk.[3]

PRAYER: Lord, I give myself to You totally. Make me a sweet savor, so others will be drawn to You. In Jesus' name. Amen.

---

3   Romans 12:1

Brief Reflection

In 2 Corinthians 2, Paul used the image of a Roman triumph. Roman triumphs were military parades. As a victorious general entered Rome, he'd lead his captured prisoners, now slaves, through its streets while sweet incense burned. Five times in his epistles, Paul referred to himself as a prisoner of Christ. When we become Christ's prisoner, we share in His triumph and victory. Are we living a victorious life?

Passages for Study

1 Corinthians 15:50-58
1 John 5:1-4

Study Notes

The Vine That Ate the South

John 15:1-11

> *I am the vine, ye are the branches: He that abideth in me, and I in him, the same bringeth forth much fruit: for without me ye can do nothing* (John 15:5, *KJV*).

The vine spreads fast as a forest fire, devouring acres and acres of farmland, climbing telephone poles and buildings, crawling over and smothering sun-starved vegetation and twining around trees. Then it plunges down river banks faster than man or grazing beast can stop it, its green leaves spreading over other plants and rocks. Is this vine invincible? Well, sometimes it seems like it. I believe we made a mistake when we imported it from China back in 1876.

Across the vast Southern landscape, it spreads. Kudzu. The only way foresters, farmers, and gardeners can rid themselves of this invasive nuisance is to kill it, every last bit, before it destroys their fruitful vegetation. Cattle help get rid of it also, by eating it. But man's battles against it seem like an endless war. Because of its aggressiveness and environmental destruction, some folks refer to it as "the vine that ate the South."

Kudzu reminds me of sin. Starting with Adam and Eve, it spread throughout the earth destroying people's souls and smothering the spiritual life out of compromising Christians.

Just as plants need the sun to thrive, so we cannot thrive without God's Son, Jesus Christ, the True Vine, shining through our lives. When we try to live righteously apart from Him, that too is sin. Only when we abide in Him will we bear holy fruit. Only when we abide in Him will we be productive in His Kingdom and victorious in our walk.

How do we abide? By sinking our spiritual roots in Him and constantly living in His presence. He's the only One who can produce righteous fruit. Let us all abide.

PRAYER: Lord God, sometimes I fail to abide in You. Sometimes I believe I can bear fruit on my own, even when I know deep in my heart that I cannot do anything without You. Forgive me for trusting in myself. I trust You, Lord. Let Your fruit shine through me. In Jesus' name. Amen.

Brief Reflection

In the natural world, of course, only good soil produces healthy plants. Jesus used the imagery of soil when He told the parable of the sower and the seed. Has His gospel seed taken root in the soil of our hearts? Are we producing good fruit? How can we do so?

Passages for Study

Matthew 13:1-9; 18-23
John 15:1-11

Study Notes

Frederic the Destroyer

Proverbs 12:1-3

A man shall not be established by wickedness: but the root of the righteous shall not be moved (Proverbs 12:3, *KJV*).

As a Gulf Coast native, I've experienced numerous hurricanes. Their fierce winds and horrific havoc have my respect, and I've always evacuated my home when warned. The meanest ones that occupy my memory? Camille, Katrina, and Frederic. In 1979, while I recuperated from a car accident in a Chattanooga hospital, Frederic slammed my hometown.

A week after the storm bashed the city my doctor released me, and my father drove me home. I gasped at Frederic's devastation. Wiped out power lines deprived Mobile of most of its electricity. Shingles and glass littered lawns and gardens. Roofless houses dared the elements to strike again. Telephone posts, ripped apart, looked like a giant's hand flung them every direction in a fit of rage. Once-majestic live oaks lay prostrate across Mobile's boulevards and streets, their thick battered trunks—uprooted, beaten, destroyed—testimony to Frederic's merciless tempest. Many months passed before the city cleared off all the debris.

Fortunately, except for losing a few shingles off its roof, my family's sturdy two-story home remained intact. Some oak trees still stood; also our palms. Their roots were strong. They could withstand anything hurled at them, even the mightiest storm's test.

God reminds us of that future day when He'll shake everything that can be shaken, so that only "those things which cannot be shaken may remain."[4]

How can we be sure, when God's Spirit blows upon the earth to separate the profitable wheat from the worthless chaff, that we'll still stand? By having our roots in the right soil, a soil called righteousness.

PRAYER: Lord Jesus, I don't want to be chaff that the wind blows away. May my roots sink deep into righteousness so that I may grow into a mature son or daughter. Thank You, Lord. In Jesus' name. Amen.

---

4   Hebrews 12:26-27

Brief Reflection

In the previous devotional, I mentioned that Jesus spoke of the soil of our hearts. In this devotional, we learned about having roots in righteous soil amidst storms and God's shaking. Jesus also spoke about hurricane-type storms that blew against houses. How were some of these houses able to stand?

Passages for Study

Matthew 7:24-29

Study Notes

Mirrors

James 1:22-25

But be ye doers of the word, and not hearers only, deceiving yourselves. For if any be a hearer of the word and not a doer, he is like unto a man beholding his natural face in a glass: For he beholdeth himself, and goeth his way, and straightway forgetteth what manner of man he was (James 1:22-24, *KJV*).

After passing through the Greater Gulf State Fair's entrance gate, my father behind me, I bumped legs and arms while I wove through a mass of noisy people. Popcorn's buttery aroma tempted my taste buds, the kernels jumping and smacking a large popcorn popper's sides. A girl licking pink cotton candy approached. *Yuk!* That junk didn't look good, not even to my adolescent, sugar-loving palate. To this day, I've never tasted it.

Once my father and I stepped into a clearer spot, I surveyed the game booths bedecked with lights as bright as an outdoor Christmas display. Beyond them, the rides. Excited squeals called to me from a roller coaster zooming up and down its undulating tracks, the Ferris wheel's slow rotation caught my attention, and bumper cars crashing into each other amidst their drivers' laughter promised excitement.

I glanced at my father. "May I go over there, sir?" I pointed at a small building bearing a sign above its door—House of Mirrors.

"That's fine," my father said.

I hurried into it and scurried from one crazy-shaped mirror to the next, chuckling at the funny reflections. One mirror stretched my small body high and narrow like a rubber band about to snap apart. Others shortened me. Some made me fire plug height. When one widened me out, I barely recognized myself. These mirrors twisted me into all kinds of humorous shapes. Of course, they didn't reflect me accurately. It was just fun.

In James's era, mirrors didn't reflect people accurately either. Made of a highly polished metal, such as bronze, these ancient mirrors only gave a person a dim image of himself or herself.

Our modern mirrors reflect our true appearance, though. Not just our exterior flaws. They show us positive things, too. If we're dressed neatly and well-groomed, we'll see this by a mirror's reflection. However, there's one thing mirrors cannot show. They cannot show our spiritual condition.

God's perfect spiritual mirror, His Word, does that. Every time we read it, we observe our spiritual reflection. Not only does it show us where we've fallen short, it also shows us where we've been obedient.

Since most of us look in a mirror every morning to make ourselves presentable to the world, it's even more important to look in God's mirror every day to be sure we're correctly representing Him to others. When His mirror shows us where we've been obedient, rejoice. When it shows us where we've fallen short, let's be sure to make things right. Let's not look into God's Word, see our faults, then forget what

He shows us. Instead, let's do His Word. We can't afford to represent Him poorly. The world is watching us.

PRAYER: Lord Jesus, when I look into the mirror of Your Word, show me where I've fallen short. By Your Holy Spirit, enable me to make things right with others when You convict me. Thank You for teaching me through Your Scriptures. In Jesus' holy name. Amen.

Brief Reflection

Though the Apostle Paul once called himself "the chief of sinners," we all fall into that category. Paul also said he exercised his conscience to keep it clear before God and before men.[5] A clear conscience means we've confessed and repented whenever we fall short of God's standard, His Word, and when we've hurt or offended others we make things right with them. Do we walk with a clear conscience every day?

Passages for Study

Psalm 32:1-11
1 John 1:5-10

Study Notes

5   Acts 24:16

A Southern Boy's Short Study: Holiness, Victory's Key

Joshua 7:1-26

And Moses said unto them, If ye will do this thing, if ye will go armed before the LORD to war, And will go all of you armed over Jordan before the LORD, until he hath driven out his enemies from before him, And the land be subdued before the LORD: then afterward ye shall return, and be guiltless before the LORD, and before Israel; and this land shall be your possession before the LORD. But if ye will not do so, behold, ye have sinned against the LORD: and be sure your sin will find you out (Numbers 32:23, *KJV*).

Israel charged across Jericho's flattened walls, its people's shouts piercing a blue sky. All about them the enemy cowered behind buildings or fled. Not one would escape. Joshua would see to that. The Lord commanded it.

Then, during the battle's tumult, a Jew named Achan spied something. Why, he couldn't believe his eyes. An expensive mantle from Shinar, a bar of gold, and two hundred shekels of silver. He was rich! Dropping his sword, his eyes darted every direction. Satisfied no one noticed, he stuffed them in his cloak and hurried to his tent. There he buried his wealth. No one would know his secret.

Next, Israel encountered Ai. A small town it was, much smaller than Jericho, so Joshua sent a portion of his army against it. One brief battle repulsed the Israelites, sent them reeling back to their camp. Ai's men pursued. Thirty-six Israelites, slain by their enemy, lay on the field.[6]

Clutching his robe, Joshua ripped it apart. He and the elders collapsed on their faces before God's ark.

"Alas, O Lord GOD," Joshua cried, "wherefore hast thou at all brought this people over Jordan, to deliver us into the hand of the Amorites, to destroy us? would to God we had been content, and dwelt on the other side Jordan."[7]

"Israel hath sinned," God told him, "and they have also transgressed my covenant which I commanded them: for they have even taken of the accursed thing, and have stolen, and dissembled also, and they have put *it* even among their own stuff."[8]

Consequently, God continued, they "could not stand before their enemies."[9]

Soon God exposed Achan's guilt. When Israel dealt with him its people could advance. After stoning him and his family, God's people conquered Ai along with other heathen towns.[10]

When we don't deal with sin, it will stop our spiritual growth. Proverbs says: "He that covereth his sins shall not prosper: but whoso confesseth and forsaketh *them* shall have

---

6   Joshua 7:1-6
7   Joshua 7:7
8   Joshua 7:11
9   Joshua 7:12
10   Joshua 7:17-26

mercy."[11] Achan concealed his sin from the world, but he couldn't hide it from God. God gives us a warning: our sin will find us out.[12]

Achan wasn't the only one who suffered for his actions. His family did, too. Sin's consequences stretch beyond us to ruin other people's lives.

David provides another good illustration. One spring year, it says in 2 Samuel 11:1, he committed adultery with Bathsheba while her husband, Uriah, was away from home fighting a war. Consequently, she became pregnant.

I know what I'll do, David thought. *I'll recall Uriah from the front.*

Upon Uriah's return, David said to him, "Go down to thy house, and wash thy feet." The Bible adds: "Uriah departed out of the king's house, and there followed him a mess *of meat* from the king."[13]

David didn't literally mean that Uriah was to wash his feet. This expression meant he was to sleep with his wife.

But Uriah didn't do this. Next day, David asked him why.

"The ark," Uriah said, "and Judah, abide in tents; and my lord Joab, and the servants of my lord, are encamped in the open fields; shall I then go into mine house, to eat and to drink, and to lie with my wife? *as* thou liveth, and as thy soul liveth, I will not do this thing."[14]

His first attempt to cover his sin having failed, David tried a different trick to get Uriah to sleep with her. He got him drunk. This didn't work, either.

David's final attempt to cover his sin? He dispatched Uriah back to the front carrying a message to General Joab,

11 Proverbs 28:13
12 Numbers 32:23
13 2 Samuel 11:8
14 2 Samuel 11:11

an order that Joab would have Uriah killed in battle by placing him in the front line. Joab obeyed; Uriah was killed.

God saw this, of course, and sent the prophet Nathan to rebuke David. He had committed a two-fold sin, adultery and murder. Though he repented, he and his family suffered its consequences:[15]

(1) The innocent son Bathesheba bore died.[16]
(2) Amnon, David's oldest son, raped his sister Tamar.[17]
(3) Absalom avenged Tamar by killing Amnon.[18]
(4) Later, Absalom led a revolt against David.[19]
(5) At the end of his revolt, Absalom was killed.[20]

If David, the man after God's own heart, could stumble, so can we. Thank goodness, we serve a God of grace who forgives! Thank goodness, for Christ's sacrifice on Calvary's cross for our sins!

When we turn from our waywardness and totally dedicate ourselves to Him we'll walk securely, our conscience clear and our hearts assured of His blessings. As we wrap our lives around Him and become intertwined with Him, we can tap into His strength to defeat Satan's wiles.

Next time temptation dangles in front of you and whispers in your ear, flee it. Fast. Flee into Jesus' mighty arms

PRAYER: Lord Jesus, let me keep my eyes focused on You, rather than the world. Thank You for enabling to resist temptation. In Your name. Amen.

---

15 2 Samuel 12:11-12
16 2 Samuel 12:18
17 2 Samuel 13:1-20
18 2 Samuel 13:28-29
19 2 Samuel 15:1-18:17
20 2 Samuel 18:14-15

Brief Reflection

When we walk in holiness, we're set apart from the world's system and live a life pleasing to God. Are we pleasing God today?

Passages for Study

1 Peter 1:13-16

Study Notes

REFLECTIONS ON MINISTRY

A Polecat in a Pig Sty

Matthew 6:1-4

Take heed that ye do not your alms before men, to be seen of them: otherwise ye have no reward of your Father which is in heaven (Matthew 6:1, *KJV*).

Where I come from, we've got a special word for skunk. What is it? Polecat. I have no idea how we Southerners came up with this word, but one evening I smelled like one. It's amazing my friends even wanted to eat my refreshments, but they did.

Well, maybe they didn't smell me. I did try to hide my odor, after all. With deodorant? With cologne? With specially-scented soap? Not that kind of odor. A spiritual odor that stank in the nostrils of almighty God. I'd just finished teaching a Bible study. Everyone arose from my living room chairs and wandered into my kitchen for snacks.

Wait! What about my lesson! Didn't anyone notice how good I was? Someone. Tell me. I know I was good!

Oops! Wrong thoughts. I rarely received compliments, and that was fine with me. But not this night. For some reason, it bothered me, so I slipped into my humility disguise and joined my friends in conversation. Humph! Who was I fooling? Certainly not the Lord. He knew my heart, just as He knew all hearts. I was "doing my righteousness before men," practicing righteousness and doing ministry to be noticed. My arrogance reeked worse than a polecat in a pig sty.

God is not impressed by eloquent sermons or fancy prayers. When we seek others' admiration our words rebound off the ceiling like a basketball off a backboard. We preach and pray to ourselves, for heaven locks its gates to such things.

When we're concerned about God's approval, though, men's opinions don't matter. Since my motives were sinful, I immediately set my heart right with Him. His eternal praise surpasses any temporal praise men may offer. True righteousness and ministry starts inward and flows outward, a byproduct of a purely motivated heart.

PRAYER: Father God, thank You for guarding my heart and showing me where my motives for service are wrong. May I always serve You with a pure heart, one that desires to please only You. In Jesus' name. Amen.

Brief Reflection

Effective ministers serve with pure hearts and motives. Those who minister with mixed motives move in pride. God only anoints and blesses the humble. In what ways can we practice humility?

Passages for Study

1 Peter 5:1-5

Study Notes

The Proud Forget

Luke 15:11-32

And he answering said to his father, Lo, these many years do I serve thee, neither transgressed I at any time thy commandment: and yet thou never gavest me a kid, that I might make merry with my friends: (Luke 15:29, *KJV*).

At age sixteen, I packed up a few of my belongings and left home. No, I wasn't a runaway. No, I wasn't kicked out of the house. No, I wasn't kidnapped. And no, I didn't do jail time. Yes, I did spend summers back home in Mobile. All right, then. What happened? I grew up during a tumultuous era, the 1960s. That's what.

As the war in Vietnam heated up and riots rocked campuses across the nation my father, who was a private pilot, and I climbed into his Beechcraft Musketeer. He flew me to the quiet town of Marion, Alabama, a spur of the moment decision we both made because of my high school's unrest. Here he enrolled me in its boarding school, Marion Military Institute. The school retains its junior college to this day. In my day, it also had a high school. My cousin, a Marine helicopter pilot who'd served a tour of duty in Vietnam, graduated from it.

For me, however, education was primary, not military goals. Also running. Though not roadrunner fast, I loved doing it. I'd tried out for the track team at one of my previous schools but didn't make the cut. Since this school let me run, I joined the cross-country team, but I'd come up here so fast I left my running shoes at home. My solution? Run barefoot till the school let me go into town to buy a pair.

Talk about a mistake! One day I fell far behind the pack as we jogged up a winding, hilly clay road. Where was I? In the very definition of the boondocks, that's where. Fear clawed me harder than an angry Alabama black bear's paw. I hoped some hunter wouldn't mistake me for a deer and take a shot at me. What about coyotes? Would they maul me? I listened for their howls.

Slowing further, I looked around. Trees, bushes, hawks circling…up ahead, the pebble-pocked road wound ever closer toward the darkening sky. Sweat coated me…not just from running…but also from nerves.

As the temperature dropped, cicadas and crickets raised a racket. The half-moon emerged onto the star-spangled stage. My spirits sagged. My calves ached as though a thousand pins had pierced them. The hard road, its rocks and pebbles, battered and bloodied my unshod feet. Still I kept running, ever slower till finally, puffing hard, I dropped to a staggering walk. How would I get back to campus? Where was it, anyway? Trouble awaited me if I ever returned, and possibly a "dishonorable discharge" from its premises.

An engine sounded behind me. Turning, I stopped. I breathed a sigh of relief. My coach pulled up alongside me in his car. I climbed in. He took me back to school. Thankfully, I didn't get into trouble.

The older brother in Jesus' parable of the prodigal son wouldn't have searched for me as my coach did. Caught up in spiritual pride and self-righteousness, he had stayed home. Content, well-fed, what did it matter to him that his lost brother might be in trouble, hurt, or, worse yet, dead?

Just as self-righteousness blinded the older brother, so it blinds us to the lost and needy. When we spend our days wearing this spiritual blindfold, our hearts harden and our memories fade. We forget our sinfulness, we forget Christ, and we live as though His sacrifice for us means nothing.

God requires humility in ministry, but when we're self-righteous we're as needy as those who are lost. May He give us the grace to show us how much we all need Him each day, and may we always have a heart to reach out to those who don't know our Savior.

PRAYER: Thank You, Lord, for sending Your only begotten Son to die for a sinner such as me. May I never forget Your sacrifice. May I walk in humility. Open my eyes that I may see those who need a Savior the way You see them. Use me, Lord, to share with them Your good news of salvation. In Jesus' name. Amen.

Brief Reflection

How easy it is for us to forget our wayward brothers and sisters! One of Paul's co-workers, Demas, went back into the world.[21] Do we know someone like Demas whom we need to rescue? Are we willing to reach out to him or her?

Passages for Study

Matthew 18:10-14

Study Notes

---

21 2 Timothy 4:9-10

Gently! Gently!

Galatians 6:1

> *Brethren, if a man be overtaken in a fault, ye which are spiritual, restore such an one in the spirit of meekness, considering thyself, lest thou also be tempted* (Galatians 6:1, *KJV*).

Strolling down my street, I relished the crisp Louisiana air. A wonderful spring day! Mockingbirds winged up into trees, cars rumbled past houses, azaleas blossomed on manicured lawns while a soft breeze bore their scent. A typical Southern day. And wonderfully hot, at least to me. Also, the perfect time for a snowball break, an interlude during my hectic schedule.

After purchasing a snowball at the stand around the corner, I headed back home. While I licked my cold treat, my thoughts roamed to other, more important things. I started across the road...*honk!* Startled by the car's horn, I leapt high, slipped on my spilled snowball, and landed smack on my face.

The squealing vehicle swerved around me and parked. Cars behind it braked.

A girl got out of her vehicle. "Are you all right?" Concerned lines tightened her face.

Still prone, I lifted my eyes toward her. "I think I am." My pride prevented me from admitting the truth. Actually, pain racked my body.

By the time I gained my feet, a young man came running toward me from the car that had honked. Apologizing profusely, he said his father meant to warn me and didn't mean to scare me. I assured them everything was fine…it wasn't…and continued the quick walk home.

Unable to move my right arm, I suspected it was broken. A friend took me to the emergency room. There, a doctor confirmed my diagnosis. When she handled my throbbing limb gently, relief rushed through me. Broken was bad enough. Had she manhandled it, the pain would've sent me screaming louder than a siren.

A similar thing happens when brothers and sisters fall into sin. They're broken, dislocated from the body of Christ. By using the word "restore," Paul painted the image of a doctor resetting a bone. Perhaps he'd seen Dr. Luke do it. When we restore an erring member of Christ's body, we're resetting them into right fellowship with God and other believers.

Like the doctor who examined my arm, we exercise gentleness during the restoration process. Restoring a fallen brother or sister isn't always easy. Not only is it painful for him or her, but also for us. Since we're all capable of falling, we have no right to manhandle verbally those who err, nor should we pass judgment. If we practice gentleness, we're being spiritually-minded. God will use us to bring healing to those willing to be restored.

PRAYER: Lord, help me to always be gentle with brothers and sisters who've stumbled, like a doctor resetting a bone. In Jesus' name. Amen.

Brief Reflection

After Jesus shared the parable of the lost sheep, the study passage in the previous devotional, He told us the pattern for restoring fallen brothers and sisters. Be careful, though. We should not use Matthew 18 as a reason to condemn folks. Restoring a brother or sister is what's important, *not* piling on condemnation. As we saw in Galatians, we must be humble and gentle during this process. Do we know someone who needs to be restored into right fellowship with God? If so, let's restore them gently.

Passages for Study

Matthew 18:15-20

Study Notes

Fiddler Faith

Romans 1:8-16

For I am not ashamed of the gospel of Christ: for it is the power of God unto salvation to every one that believeth; to the Jew first, and also to the Greek (Romans 1:16, *KJV*).

On the Gulf of Mexico's beaches small creatures skitter every direction. Surf fishermen and other beach visitors generally ignore them. These busy creatures always act like they're fleeing the human race. In reality, they're fleeing the incoming tide. Their ten tiny legs carry them across the sand pretty fast. As quickly as they can, they scoot into burrows they've dug.

What are these creatures? Fiddler crabs, called this because the male fiddler's one oversized claw reminds us of a violinist as it moves up and down as though playing the instrument. Harmless creatures, they're sometimes sold in pet stores. Their burrows serve many purposes, not only to escape high tide, but also for laying eggs and providing a refuge from predators.

My numerous trips to the beach and observations of these creatures have often sent my thoughts drifting toward my Christian testimony. Am I hiding in a "burrow," seeking refuge from human predators who oppose my faith? Do I have a fiddler crab kind of faith?

We Christians can't afford this. We can't afford to fear predators and persecution's incoming tides. Fiddler faith Christians burrow in their "safe zones." Secret Christians with a secret faith, they dare not speak out about Christ and His Word lest they offend someone or suffer as a consequence.

Yet the Apostle Paul says the gospel will offend people. In his letter to the Galatians, he called it the "offence of the cross."[22] Had the early church's leaders been "fiddler faith" Christians, the church never would've been born. God's Holy Spirit empowered them with boldness to preach His Word.

Since His Holy Spirit also lives inside us, we too can be bold. Let's not harbor our faith in secret nor flee the worldly tide by scurrying into our burrows. Christianity shouldn't be a clique where everyone gathers into their safe zones. Rather, it should advance toward the high tide of a needy humanity, bringing Christ to everyone.

PRAYER: Fill me with boldness, Lord, that I may not be intimidated by the world or its ways. In Jesus' name. Amen.

---

22 Galatians 5:11

Brief Reflection

After Jesus' crucifixion, the disciples went into hiding. After His resurrection and ascension into Heaven, the Holy Spirit filled them with boldness on the day of Pentecost. Likewise, we can't be bold in ourselves. We need His Holy Spirit to empower us to spread His gospel. If we know Him as our Lord and Savior, He's given us this power. Will we trust His enablement to go forth and spread His good news of salvation?

Passages for Study

Acts 1:4-8
Acts 2:1-4
Acts 4:23-31

Study Notes

Free Fried Fish

Luke 6:37-38

> *Give, and it will be given unto you; good measure, pressed down, and shaken together, and running over, shall men give into your bosom. For with the same measure that ye mete withal it shall be measured to you again* (Luke 6:38, *KJV*).

My father and a friend often held free fish fries for various charities in and around Mobile. Sometimes, I'd help out. Even while I pen these words, cooking oil and fish batter saturate my memory. The sizzles of mackerel and trout we tossed into the propane-powered deep fryers revisit my recollections.

My most vivid memory, though, were folks' smiling faces and happy chatter as they lined up for fish and hush puppies. Nothing like free seafood straight out of the Gulf of Mexico!

My father and I usually caught most of it. On days when our anglers' luck didn't hold, my father bought the fish. Also, he received donations from others. Our connections with local commercial fishermen helped out as well.

One midnight phone call awakened my father, an offer and a request. If he'd come down to the docks and help clean a grouper, he could have it. Of course, he went. That fish was almost as long as he was tall, evidenced by a photograph of the fish dangling off a post secured by a large hook and line, my five-foot ten father standing beside it. Our fish were always fresh.

Though my father's dental practice and hobbies demanded much of his time, he didn't neglect this special opportunity to serve others. He knew how to schedule his activities. Giving money is important, no doubt about that, but I daresay giving time can sometimes be a greater sacrifice. How easy it is for us to make excuses.

Are some excuses legitimate? Of course! But in many cases saying, "I'm too busy," is an easy way to avoid serving others. As with my father, we're all busy. It's not a matter of *having* the time; it's often a matter of *making* the time to be a servant.

True, sometimes we must say "no" to certain activities, nor can we always expect to be available for every opportunity that lands at our doorstep, nor can we always answer every plea. Burnout affects us all.

However, if saying, "I'm too busy," is an excuse to avoid a sacrifice of time, we don't understand true ministry. True ministry involves service, and service requires sacrifice. God, in return, will bless us, because by serving others we also serve Him. I believe the greatest blessing, though, is the joy we experience through service.

PRAYER: Dear Lord, teach me how to manage my time. Make me a willing servant who always makes time for others in need. In Jesus' name. Amen.

Brief Reflection

We cannot serve the Lord by living in our own little worlds, isolated from folks and doing our own thing. Do we serve others?

Passages for Study

Matthew 25:31-46
James 2:14-26
Romans 15:1-6

Study Notes

A Southern Boy's Short Study:
A Brass Thing

2 Kings 18:1-8

> *He removed the high places, and brake the images, and cut down the groves, and brake in pieces the brasen serpent that Moses had made: for unto those days the children of Israel did burn incense to it: and he called it Nehushtan* (2 Kings 18:4, *KJV*).

Every time I visited my grandmother, a certain brass thing sat on her bedroom's writing desk. As a child, I sometimes played with it. Upon her passing when I was in my twenties I got possession of it, an owl standing atop a short ruler. A paperweight, actually. But what does a brass thing have to do with the Lord?

Well, God told Moses to make one during Israel's wilderness wanderings. This event is recorded in Numbers 21:4-9. While the Israelites bypassed Edom impatience, manifested through their grumbling and complaining, got the better of them. They said to Moses: "…Wherefore have ye brought us up out of Egypt to die in the wilderness? For *there is* no bread, neither *is there any* water, and our soul loatheth this light bread."[23]

23 Numbers 21:5

God gave them manna, also water out of a rock, yet they complained. Nothing satisfied them.

Consequently, He sent fiery serpents into their midst.[24] Whenever they bit a person, that person died. Scholars have theorized on what species of snakes these were; we'll not discuss that here. The important thing is this: We commit a serious sin when we complain about the One who totally loves us. When we complain about the human leadership He's given us, like the Israelites grumbling against Moses, we're also complaining against Him.

Because of these serpents, the people "...came to Moses and said, We have sinned, for we have spoken against the LORD, and against thee; pray unto the LORD, that he take away the serpents from us. And Moses prayed for the people."[25]

During Moses' intercession God told him to make a fiery serpent out of brass "and set it upon a pole: and it shall come to pass, that everyone that is bitten, when he looketh upon it, shall live. And Moses made a serpent of brass, and put it upon a pole, and it came to pass, that if a serpent had bitten any man, when he beheld the serpent of brass, he lived."[26]

Pondering this episode, I wondered. Brass? A serpent? Why? My pondering led to this understanding: 1) The people confessed their sin of murmuring against the Lord and against Moses, 2) God used the serpent, a biblical symbol of evil,[27] to represent their sin, and 3) because of its ability to endure fire, brass represents God's judgment.[28] God's message to them, then, was that He'd judged their sin. Only one thing

---

24 Numbers 21:6
25 Numbers 21:7
26 Numbers 21:8-9
27 Genesis 3:1-5
28 Revelation 1:15

did He require. To be healed, the people had to express their faith by looking at it.

Since the Lord condemned idolatry and the making of idols,[29] He only meant this brass thing to be symbolic. But by King Hezekiah's day many centuries later, the people of Judah were worshipping it, burning incense to it. Hezekiah called it Nehushtan, a brass thing, because that's exactly what it was. [30] Wisely, he destroyed it.

Why had the people made this brass thing an idol? Why do folks make anything an idol? Could it be because they no longer hunger and thirst after God? Could it be because the world has trapped them in an eternal rat race, chasing one temporal pleasure after another only to find permanent satisfaction elusive? Actually, to find permanent satisfaction, all they have to do is turn back to God.

Let's take this thought further. Though God did use the brass serpent in the past, the people in Hezekiah's day believed He still used it, but He didn't. If we're always dwelling on God's glorious moves of yesteryear, constantly talking about the "good ole days," we're actually worshipping His past deeds instead of looking for Him to move in the here and now. When we live in the past, our vision for revival in our own day fades to nothing.

The brass serpent wasn't a bad thing at first. Likewise, God's gifts and callings and ministries are good. Nevertheless, good things can become idols. Worship, church buildings, church music, Sunday school classes, church leaders, and many other positive things can lead to idolatry. It's a grave error to idolize the ministries He's given others. When we do this, we worship his or her gifts instead of the Giver Himself.

---

29 Exodus 20:4
30 2 Kings 18:4

Worshiping human leaders—that's what cults do. It's also a grave error to idolize the ministries He's given us. When we do, it leads to pride.

Do we have Nehushtans in our lives? Get rid of them, destroy them like King Hezekiah and worship God alone. Visit John 3 next, where Christ explained the brass thing's symbolism: "And as Moses lifted up the serpent in the wilderness, even so must the Son of man be lifted up: That whosoever believeth in him should not perish, but have eternal life."[31]

Christ judged our sin on Calvary. The brass serpent pointed to Him. Let's not take our salvation lightly. He paid the ultimate price for us. He alone should be worshiped. No brass thing, no idol, can compare with Him and His work on Calvary's cross.

PRAYER: Dear Lord, forgive me for placing other things in my life ahead of You. You alone are worthy of my worship. In Jesus' name. Amen.

31 John 3:14-15

Brief Reflection

The thing we love most is the thing that takes first place in our hearts. Does God sit upon our heart's throne, or does something else?

Passages for Study

Leviticus 19:4-8
1 John 5:21
Psalm 115

Study Notes

REFLECTIONS ON WARFARE

Be Alert

1 Peter 5:1-9

Be sober, be vigilant; because your adversary the devil, as a roaring lion, walketh about, seeking whom he may devour: Whom resist stedfast in the faith, knowing that the same afflictions are accomplished in your brethren that are in the world (1 Peter 5:8-9, *KJV*).

Winter nipped my bare hands while I sat beneath a tree, my shotgun cradled in my lap. Though the sun still lingered in the sky, afternoon was winding down. Surely a deer would show up soon. But the minutes grew longer, my patience shorter. A fox darted past me, fleeing some other hunter's dog hot on his tail. An occasional squirrel ventured near.

Then I spotted him, a whitetail deer wandering toward me. *Aha! Right within my range.* I snapped off my safety. The deer stopped. *Uh-oh.* I'd made my presence known. Our gazes locked. Did he see me behind the bush? Holding my breath, I hoped he'd come closer still. Seconds later he bounded off and through the brush.

I leapt from my hiding place, triggered two wild shots… the deer sprinted safely away. I yelled at myself. Some great hunter this Southern boy was. I am a far better saltwater fisherman than hunter, I'd say.

Fortunately for the deer, he was alert. His keen ears helped him detect an enemy.

Satan, our enemy, either walks about "like a roaring lion" or lies in wait to snare us. By keeping our spiritual ears alert, we'll hear the Holy Spirit's warnings when our foe sets his traps, just as my clicking safety alerted that deer.

How do we stay alert? This comes through prayer, through meditation on His Word, through waiting before Him and listening for His still, small voice. In essence, through daily fellowship with Him.

PRAYER: Dear Lord Jesus, may my ears stay attuned to Your still small voice, guiding me into Your will and alerting me to the enemy's snares. Thank You, Lord. In Your most holy name. Amen.

Brief Reflection

When we expose our eyes and minds to ungodly things, and listen to the world clamoring for our attention, we become deaf to God's Holy Spirit. Through fellowship with our Savior, we find strength and the ability to hear His still, small voice. Do we listen for His voice every day?

Passages for Study

1 Kings 19:9-13

Study Notes

What My Cat Taught Me

Numbers 13:26-33

And there we saw the giants, the sons of Anak, which come of the giants: and we were in our own sight as grasshoppers, and so we were in their sight (Numbers 13:33, *KJV*).

Behind my childhood home runs an alley. From this alley, stray cats often wandered onto our property where my mother always fed them. Alley cats they were, in the strictest sense, so it's no wonder that I adopted a stray who wandered onto my lawn in Kenner, Louisiana.

A beautiful gray kitty with a gentle temperament, she was the perfect pet. I named her Koshka, Russian for female cat, I'd learned in my college's Russian class. One day, though, a neighbor looked down at her and said to me, "Your cat looks pregnant."

Pregnant! The word gripped my throat. That was the last thing I needed. I could afford Koshka, but care for a litter of kittens? *Oh, no!* For several days, I studied Koshka's swollen belly. Mews and meows of imaginary kittens wreaked havoc on my brain's "movie screen." What would happen after she gave birth? Happen? To her? To her kittens? What about me? My bank account? My money?

Every day, visions of dwindling finances dominated my concerns. Anxieties intensified. I wanted to scream: "Koshka, girl, why are you doing this to me?"

Finally, I took her to the veterinarian to verify her pregnancy.

After his examination, he announced the verdict. "She's not pregnant. She's been spayed. She's just fat."

Whew! All my nervous tension broke at his announcement. Peace swept over and through me like a gurgling stream.

But isn't this what the enemy does to us if we let him? After Moses' twelve spies returned from scouting out Canaan, panic seized ten of them. They couldn't take the land. Giants were there, "and we were in our own sight as grasshoppers, and so we were in their sight." First Satan planted doubt in their minds, then faithlessness supplanted faith and finally, an overactive imagination produced an overwhelming terror. Because they believed what they saw and listened to the enemy's lie, they missed God's blessing.

Not so two others spies, Caleb and Joshua. God told them He'd give them the land, and they believed it. They listened to His Word. When the day finally arrived, they marched into the Promised Land, the last survivors of Moses' generation.

Because I listened to the authority regarding Koshka, I gained peace of mind. Likewise, when we listen to and heed God's authority, His Word, the Lord will lead us to victory through every battle just as He did Caleb and Joshua.

PRAYER: Dear Lord, I believe Your Word, the only authority for how I should live my life. Thank You for it, and for the peace You give me when I listen to and obey You. May I continue heeding Your guidance. Help me to ignore the enemy's lies. In Jesus' name. Amen.

Brief Reflection

When we listen to Satan's negative thoughts, we allow him to steal our faith. Do we believe God's promises and walk in faith like Caleb and Joshua?

Passages to Study

John 8:33-47
John 6:34-40

Study Notes

Whom Do You Follow?

2 Corinthians 11:1-15

> *But what I do, that I will do, that I may cut off occasion from them which desire occasion; that wherein they glory, they may be found even as we. For such are false apostles, deceitful workers, transforming themselves into the apostles of Christ. And no marvel; for Satan himself is transformed into an angel of light. Therefore it is no great thing if his ministers also be transformed as the ministers of righteousness; whose end shall be according to their works* (2 Corinthians 11:12-15, *KJV*).

My brother-in-law's white pickup roared ahead, leading me toward his cotton farm on a warm summer day. Though I'd never driven there before, following him was easy; that is, till we reached the traffic light on the edge of town.

Seconds after he passed beneath its green light, it flicked red. He kept on his way. I braked and waited and assured myself that I'd catch up. But by the time it changed green, he'd sped well out of sight. I clenched my steering wheel tighter. Narrow country road stretched miles ahead. No trucks, no cars, nothing. I had no idea where I was. "Great. Now what am I going to do?"

I suddenly breathed easier, for I saw it—the distant white pickup racing past pine trees and cotton fields. I accelerated; the truck accelerated. I gained more speed; so did the truck. I fumed. *Why is he going so fast? I can't afford a speeding ticket. We're only going to a picnic.*

At an intersection, the pickup made a sharp left down another road. My thoughts froze; my spirits sagged. I gulped. "Great. Just great." I'd never been here before, not even with my sister. My gas gauge's needle approached empty. I slowed, noticed a nice neighborhood on my left, and turned down its street where I parked. Slumped against my steering wheel, I berated myself. Lost. I'd followed the wrong white pickup. The only thing I figured was that somehow, while I waited at the red light, that truck had entered in front of me from a side road I didn't see, and though it looked like my brother-in-law's vehicle, it wasn't. I'd failed to keep close to him.

I called my sister on my cell phone. "Lynn, I have no idea what happened."

"Where are you?" she said, her voice frantic. "We're all waiting for you."

"I'm fine. I just have no idea where I am." I gave her the name of the street that I'd turned onto and a brief description of what happened.

"I'll send Myles to get you."

"Thanks." Sighing, I clicked off my phone.

Minutes later, my nephew Myles arrived in his truck and led me in the right direction. While I followed him, my thoughts wandered back to Paul's warning about false teachers and how that wrong white truck reminded me of them. Paul called these ministers of Satan "false apostles, deceitful workers, transforming themselves into apostles of Christ." On the outside, they look and sound like true

Christians, but they preach another Jesus, a different gospel from the true one, and lead others astray.

"I'd better be more careful," I told myself as I turned through my brother-in-law's opened gate. As I got out of my car, I determined to be more diligent in personal Bible study. I didn't want a false teacher leading me astray as that white pickup had done.

PRAYER: Lord Jesus, give me a greater hunger for You and Your Word, that I might be more diligent in the study of Your Word. In Jesus' name. Amen.

Brief Reflection

Just as it was in Paul's day, false teachers are all around us. The Bible gives us guidelines on how to spot them. How are people deceived today?

Passages for Study

1 John 4:1-6
Luke 6:24-26
1 Thessalonians 2:1-12

Study Notes

The Know-it-All

Ephesians 4:1-3

With all lowliness and meekness, with longsuffering, forbearing one another in love; Endeavouring to keep the unity of the Spirit in the bond of peace (Ephesians 4:2-3, *KJV*).

"All you need is aspirin." Ten years old and sitting in the backseat of my father's car, I argued with him.

"No, Jack." My father slowed to a stop at a red light. "Sometimes we dentists have to do root canals and sometimes we have to pull a patient's tooth. If the tooth—"

"Nuh-uh! Just give your patients aspirins when they have a toothache. That's all they need."

Exasperated, my father slapped his steering wheel. "You ought to be a lawyer. You'll argue about things you know nothing about."

This silenced me. All right, I confess. I don't really recall our argument's topic, but I do recall our trip to Birmingham, Alabama and my father's words of rebuke. As sure as hens lay eggs, I'd argue about everything till they quit laying them. And after they quit laying them, I'd argue even more. A know-it-all first class. That was me.

My argumentative spirit accompanied me into my adult years. After I became a Christian, I debated other believers on biblical doctrine. It became a pastime, both for me and for them. Sometimes tempers flared and we'd dig in our heels regarding our beliefs. When the debate ended, almost without fail, I suffered aftereffects—exhaustion, emptiness, irritability.

What had arguing accomplished? Nothing.

Who had I edified by arguing? No one.

How had arguing promoted unity in Christ's church and the spread of the gospel? It hadn't.

Many years later my arguing slowed and eventually stopped. Oh, that's not to say I've stopped entirely. From time to time, I've still stumbled into Satan's debate trap. The enemy loves it when we Christians snipe at each other. It creates disharmony, shatters our witness, hinders revival, and brings defeat.

Armies who aren't united in purpose can't win battles. Neither can Christ's army, the church, when it doesn't march together against its common enemy, the devil. As Christian soldiers, let's remember David's words: "Behold, how good and how pleasant *it is* for brethren to dwell together in unity!"[32]

I've experienced the truth of these words. It's far more productive to seek peace, encouraging our brothers and sisters, than it is to tear them down and indulge our pride by proving to ourselves that we "know it all."

The mighty Lord God, He is the only One who possesses all knowledge. We don't have to be right all the time. After all, we're human, and He is God.

PRAYER: Make me into a peace-loving person, Lord. Help me strive for unity in Your church. Help me love others, even those with whom I disagree. In Jesus' name. Amen.

---

32 Psalm 133:1, *KJV*

Brief Reflection

When the church is divided and her members argue, the enemy can gain a foothold among them and create havoc. How can we promote unity in the body of Christ?

Passages for Study

Psalm 133:1-3
1 Corinthians 1:10-16
Romans 14:13-23

Study Notes

Four Men and the Sea

James 5:13-18

Confess your faults one to another, and pray one for another, that ye may be healed. The effectual fervent prayer of a righteous man availeth much (James 5: 16, KJV).

Wheee! Shree! My father's fishing line screamed when a fish snatched his bait. It yanked his rod and almost jerked him into the Gulf of Mexico before he started reeling it in. Two of his friends and I watched, wondering what he'd caught. Whatever it was, it wasn't a Spanish mackerel. This baby fought like his life depended on it—and it did.

Anxious minutes passed. The fish kept the upper fin. Whenever my father spelled himself from his battle... *shree!* The fish shot through the waves at greyhound speed. Slumping on the boat's seat, Dad soon passed me the rod.

I resumed the fight. The rod bent sharply, almost an arc. Its tip touched the water. I wound the reel, grunting and groaning and clenching my teeth. Pain sliced my muscles during our fierce tug-of-war. I paused for a breather. *Whee! Shree!* The fish plowed the waves farther out than before.

Bone-exhausted, I passed the rod to the next man, whom the fish likewise wore out. He passed it to fisherman number four, who after his battle, returned the rod to my father.

Almost an hour had elapsed, or so it seemed, and though the fish stayed on the hook we'd not pulled him any closer. Now rested, my father managed to bring him in after one final, climatic fight.

"Jack cavalla," he said, dragging it over our craft's gunwales.

I wished we'd weighed it. Cavallas can grow as large and heavy as fifty pounds. I doubt ours weighed that much, because if it did it would've probably been a record catch.

Cavallas, also called jack crevalles or crevalle jacks, aren't as delectable as mackerel or trout. Because they're notorious fighters, though, they're fun to catch. Our determined, fervent effort to bring him in reminds me of James's words: "The effectual, fervent prayer of a righteous man availeth much." Fervent prayer equals determined prayer. Determination drove us to keep reeling till we finally brought in our catch. Likewise, fervent prayer doesn't stop till the answer comes.

James continued: "Elias was a man subject to like passions as we are, and he prayed earnestly that it might not rain: and it rained not on the earth by a space of three years and six months. And he prayed again, and the heaven gave rain, and the earth brought forth her fruit."[33]

Have we ever quit praying for something because we didn't see visible results? Suppose Elijah gave up after his second prayer? Would rain have come? What if my father, due to his exhaustion, had just cut his fishing line and let the cavalla go free? We'd have never had the pleasure of victory over him after our "heroic" battle, nor would I have the photograph of me holding it, nor would we have enjoyed a cavalla dinner that night.

---

33 James 5:17-18

This photo not only brings back this warm memory, it also reminds me to persevere in prayer. When we pray, we're not just talking to God, we're also engaged in spiritual warfare. This is why James encourages us to persevere.

PRAYER: Make me an Elijah, Lord. Help me to wrestle in prayer during spiritual battles and never cease till, in Your good and perfect time, Your answer comes. In Jesus' name. Amen.

Brief Reflection

Don't be surprised at the enemy's attacks when we engage in fervent intercessory prayer. He would like us to quit praying, because such prayer is effective. When we're tempted to quit the battle, that's when answers are around the corner. Do we quit in the midst of the battle, or do we see it through to its victorious end?

Passages for Study

Genesis 18:16-33
1 Kings 18:42-46
Acts 12:6-19

Study Notes

A Southern Boy's Short Study: God's Armor

Ephesians 6:11-20

Put on the whole armour of God, that ye may be able to stand against the wiles of the devil (Ephesians 6:11, *KJV*).

When I first learned about them in the fourth grade, Spanish explorers captured my imagination, especially since they journeyed through my home state.

One such explorer, Hernando De Soto, led his small army of six hundred soldiers against ten thousand Maubilian warriors. After a nine hour battle he broke these natives' grip on power and torched their capital village, Maubila.

How could such a small number of soldiers defeat these thousands? The Spaniards wielded superior weapons and wore armor, whereas the Maubilians wore no armor and wielded mere spears and arrows.

Satan and his myriad demonic host will attack us, it is certain, but God has equipped us with superior weapons. Also, spiritual armor. Satan is naked, defeated, his power broken by Jesus Christ. Our warfare isn't a worldly conflict, Paul says, but a spiritual one.[34]

34 Ephesians 6:12

To stand against him, we must don God's whole armor, every piece of it, every day. Paul wrote to the Ephesian believers: "Wherefore take unto you the whole armour of God, that ye may be able to withstand in the evil day, and having done all, to stand."[35]

Paul then details our armor's equipment. The first two pieces? The belt and the breastplate. "Stand therefore, having your loins girt about with truth, and having on the breastplate of righteousness," he wrote. [36]

In Paul's day Roman soldiers wore girdles, or belts, around their breastplates. Belt-plates fastened the belts and soldiers wore their swords (sometimes also daggers) on them. One other useful thing about a soldier's belt—he could tuck his knee-length tunic into it whenever he needed to.

Wearing our spiritual belt requires three things: (1) an intimate relationship with the Truth, Jesus Christ; (2) a solid grounding in sound doctrine as found in God's training manual, the Bible; and (3) applying its truth to our daily lives. Truth is the foundation for our living and service. Without it, we cannot wax victorious in battle.

The second piece is the "breastplate of righteousness." The Roman soldier's most common breastplate, as used in the first Christian century, consisted of two iron plates connected by leather straps. It protected the soldier's chest and back between his neck and stomach.

Paul alluded to each half in 1 Thessalonians 5:8 when he told believers to put on "the breastplate of faith and love." God justifies (declares righteous) those who live by faith.[37] This means we're in right standing with Him. When we love others, we're living a practical life of righteousness because

35 Ephesians 6:13
36 Ephesians 6:14
37 Romans 1:17

love fulfills the Law.[38] When we walk by faith and practice love, we've strapped on our breastplate.

The next piece Paul mentioned? A soldier's footwear. "And your feet shod with the preparation of the gospel of peace," he told them.[39] As he marched over his empire's concrete roads and rugged terrain, the Roman soldier's hobnailed sandals gave his feet firmer traction. Made of either ox or cowhide, their durability enabled him to go virtually anywhere for a long time without needing new footwear.

Similarly, when we shod our feet with the "preparation of the gospel of peace" we're ready to march anywhere God sends us, into any place or situation no matter what its spiritual or earthly terrain. We're always ready to share His Word, and we can say with the prophet Isaiah, "Here *am* I; send me."[40]

Ah, now the soldier's dressed. He's grounded in truth, walking in righteousness, and has his gospel shoes on. Next, he grasps his shield: "Above all, taking the shield of faith, wherewith ye shall be able to quench all the fiery darts of the wicked."[41]

The Roman foot soldier's shield, rectangular in shape and curved, protected most of his body from enemy projectiles. Our shield, faith, protects us by deflecting and quenching the enemy's fiery ammunition. Though he may hurl doubt, confusion, depression, temptation and myriad other things at us, when our faith is strong and sure, we can advance against him, confidently knowing God is with us. Try as he will, the enemy's ammo can't affect us when we carry our shields.

---

38 Romans 13:10
39 Ephesians 6:15
40 Isaiah 6:8
41 Ephesians 6:16

Of course, soldiers can't enter battle with their heads unprotected. If they do, they're only asking for trouble. A Roman helmet protected most of the soldier's head—his neck, forehead, and cheeks.

Our helmet is called the "helmet of salvation"[42] or as Paul told the Thessalonians, the helmet of the "hope of salvation."[43] Hope? Does that mean crossing our fingers waiting for something to happen? No, indeed. Biblical hope is confidence in the Lord and His salvation, both in the here and now as well as in the future when He delivers us from the presence of sin to spend eternity with Him. No matter how fierce our fight, when we wear this helmet, we have confidence in the Lord.

His helmet now protecting his head, the soldier picks up his offensive weapon, his short sword. Sheathing it, he's prepared to advance against the enemy in close combat and drive him back. Paul called it "the sword of the Spirit, which is the word of God."[44]

In Matthew 4:1-11 our Lord and Savior used it against the enemy in the wilderness, a spiritual fencing contest that drove Satan away along with his temptations. Satan quoted scripture, and Christ responded back with scripture. Christ used the *rhema* word against the enemy, that is, individual scriptures from the *logos,* the entire written Word of God.

Since Satan knows the Bible, how much more should we. If we don't know God's Word, we're setting ourselves up for him to twist it to his own destructive ends. But when we know God's Word, when we've stored His Word in our hearts, His Holy Spirit will quicken His *rhemas* to us when we need

---

42 Ephesians 6:17
43 1 Thessalonians 5:8
44 Ephesians 6:17

them. Wielding them, we can rip asunder our enemy's lies. We can defeat him on the field of battle.

Finally, Paul adds that in addition to wearing the armor, we must pray always.[45] Pray as we put on our armor, pray throughout our day. Prayer, as though the sword of the Spirit, is a powerful offensive weapon. Through it, we can find the strength to stand in the midst of our hottest battles.

These thoughts on God's armor are the reflections of a simple Alabama boy who knows that much more can be said on the subject. I will conclude this way: always be aware that we have a foe who will never cease trying to stop us from doing God's will, but by donning God's armor every day he can't touch us. Christ won the victory. We're fighting a defeated foe. Amen.

PRAYER: Dear Lord, I am putting on every piece of Your armor today. I am ready to go out into the world as your soldier, to win others to Your Son, Jesus Christ. Amen.

---

45   Ephesians 6:18

Brief Reflection

When we're being effective in God's kingdom, advancing the cause of the gospel, Satan will always try to stop us. Are we wearing every piece of our armor when we go out into the world?

Passages for Study

Romans 13:11-14

Study Notes

REFLECTIONS ON GOD'S BLESSINGS

The Piano

Hebrews 6:9-15

That ye be not slothful, but followers of them who through faith and patience inherit the promises (Hebrews 6:12, KJV).

The upright piano stands in my living room. I don't play it but my grandmother, an elementary school teacher, did, at home and in silent movie theaters.

Though she passed away when I was in the sixth grade, this piano holds one special memory. At the end of every visit with her and my grandfather, she'd sit at it and play the "Smokey the Bear Song." My sister and I always sang it. Her gentle face aglow, her fingers deftly moving up and down the keyboard, she joined our singing. We both cherish this family ritual. After so many decades, we can still sing the lyrics.

For more than twenty years I waited for this piano, my inheritance my mother passed on to me. Valid reasons delayed my receiving it. Through this long waiting period I often worried. Sure, it was just a material thing. For me, however, it presented the most vivid memory of my grandmother, and therein lay its importance.

Numerous setbacks, many doubts...I gave up ever getting it. Finally, the day arrived. Movers brought it into my house, my wonderful inheritance, my grandmother's picture atop it.

Alas, Abraham's faith exceeded mine. He waited for God's promise far longer than me. God kept His Word. Through faith and patience "he obtained the promise" that God would bless him, multiply him, give him a son—his inheritance.

Circumstances said it was impossible. He was old. His wife, Sarah, was beyond the age of childbearing. Yet God came through and Sarah gave birth to their son Isaac.

So why did I start thinking I wouldn't receive my grandmother's piano? Because I focused on my circumstances, that is, the valid reasons and things that delayed its arrival. When we focus on the wrong things, we open our heart's door and say, "Come on in, doubt. Sit a while." Which is what I did.

We have no reason to doubt God. He promises us that if we, like Abraham, wait patiently and continue in faith, we'll obtain our inheritance. May we never lose our focus. Our loving God is faithful. He *always* keeps His Word.

PRAYER: Thank You, heavenly Father, for all of Your promises. May I always keep my eyes on You and know that no matter what my circumstances are, You will keep Your Word and always come through. In Jesus' name. Amen.

Brief Reflection

Earthly inheritances and worldly possessions are fine, but once we die, we leave everything we own to others. Our spiritual inheritances are eternal; therefore, far more valuable than the world's. Do we value our heavenly inheritance?

Passages for Study

1 Peter 1:1-4
2 Corinthians 5:1-5
Revelation 21:1-8

Study Notes

The Nearsighted, Farsighted Man

Deuteronomy 23:3-5

Nevertheless the LORD thy God would not hearken unto Balaam; but the LORD thy God turned the curse into a blessing unto thee, because the LORD thy God loved thee (Deuteronomy 23:5, *KJV*).

I scanned my living room. Its maroon love seat, black floor lamp, and oak coffee table swam like fuzzy fish. Next, I removed my eyeglasses. Gone the blurs, as their colors, lines, and shapes focused. "Hey. What's going on?"

Stepping outside my house, I gazed down my street. Nearby stop signs and trees stood sharp. Not so, the distant things. I couldn't even read numbers on houses. Because I'm farsighted, I knew something wasn't right. I phoned an optometrist, scheduled an appointment, and bought drugstore glasses to help me see.

A week later, after he examined me, he said, "Do you have a history of diabetes in your family?"

Strange question. "No," I said.

"Well, your vision has obviously changed. You're no longer farsighted. You've become nearsighted. I'll write you a prescription for new glasses. Meantime, I want you to see your primary care physician and make another appointment to see me."

So I made my new appointment with him, walked to the optician next door to have my prescription filled, then returned home. I phoned my main doctor.

Once I explained what happened, his nurse checked my glucose. Way over three hundred. I thought nothing of this till he announced his diagnosis. "Diabetes."

This slammed me like a pro wrestler hurling me onto a wrestling mat. What was worse, he immediately put me in the hospital to get my glucose under control. Before my release, I met with the hospital's dietician. She gave me a long list of things I could and could not eat.

"Great." I got into my car, started its engine, and backed out of my spot. "Just great. No more ice cream."

Back home, I tossed the dietician's menu on my dining table. This was no way for a sugar-happy person like me to live.

My disappointment has since faded out of existence. No longer do I consider diabetes a curse. Rather, perhaps even strangely, it's become a blessing. I've learned it can be managed.

The real blessing, though, is this—because of my diabetes I must eat right and exercise. Eating right and exercise promotes a healthier lifestyle, a far cry different from my previous unhealthy habits. The Lord took my diabetes curse and turned it into a blessing. Look for His blessing in every situation. Our God is good.

PRAYER: Dear Lord, help me to see Your love and blessing in every situation I encounter. Thank You that You can turn what may seem a curse into a blessing. In Jesus' name. Amen.

Brief Reflection

Joseph's story provides a wonderful example of God's providence and provision during a difficult time—a famine. After Joseph's brothers sold him into slavery, everything looked bleak. But eventually, the Lord raised him up to be second only to pharaoh. In Genesis 45, Joseph tells his brothers how God had engineered his situation. What first seemed a curse (Joseph's slavery) turned into a blessing. Do we look for God's hand and His blessing in our situations?

Passages for Study

Genesis 45:1-15

Study Notes

Persecution

Matthew 5:10-12

Blessed are ye, when men shall revile you, and persecute you, and shall say all manner of evil against you falsely, for my sake (Matthew 5:11, *KJV*).

Because I'm a Deep South Southern boy, I grew up in the Bible Belt. Churches are on every corner (well, almost, it seems like). The gospel message wasn't new to me, nor was persecution a common occurrence. Only after I gave my heart to Christ in the early 1970s did I experience it in its mildest form—name calling and mockery.

One day I started reading about believers in the Soviet Union and other oppressive countries. In these lands, our brothers and sisters suffered horrendous things—imprisoned in gulags, tortured and executed for their faith. It was a far cry from what we American Christians endured.

As our country entered the twenty-first century, persecution amped up and ambushed believers in many pockets of our great land. Lawsuits against Christian businesses, social media hate fests, false accusations. I could continue, but let's hear Jesus' words on this subject.

When He used the word "persecution" in His Sermon on the Mount, He meant "to put to flight, to drive away, to pursue." We are the "salt of the earth," He went on to say in Matthew 5:13.

For centuries people used salt as a preservative. But we Christians can only be savory salt when we walk in righteousness. Ungodly folks (and Satan, our enemy) don't care about compromising Christians, nor do they worry about the lukewarm. The ungodly only hate those who take a stand for Truth.

Christians who please their Savior preserve their society's culture. This threatens scoffers. By driving away and silencing God's children, scoffers think they'll have more freedom to spread their sinful ways. Through persecution they hope, in vain, to vanquish us.

It shouldn't come as a surprise, then, when Jesus said that the world would hate us: "If the world hate you, ye know that it hated me before *it hated* you."[46] What an honor, to be treated the way our Savior was!

Honor? Blessing? How can that be? Jesus said that those who are persecuted for His name have a great reward in heaven.[47] Eternal rewards far exceed any earthly reward. After all, earthly rewards pass away. Therefore, persecution is a blessing. When people hate us because of our faith, God honors us because we're following Jesus.

Been persecuted lately? Rejoice!

PRAYER: Thank You, Lord, for those times when I'm persecuted. Let me see them as an honor and a sign that I am pleasing You. In Jesus' name. Amen.

---

46 John 15:18
47 Matthew 5:12

Brief Reflection

When we're totally dedicated to the Lord, expect persecution. Persecution not only means we're doing something right, it also means we're pleasing the Lord. Have we considered persecution a blessing?

Passages for Study

Luke 6:22-23
John 15:18-25
2 Corinthians 4:7-18

Study Notes

Storm Bird

Jeremiah 17:7-8

Blessed is the man that trusteth in the LORD, and whose hope the LORD is (Jeremiah 17:7, *KJV*).

Hurricane Frederic was bad enough, as was Hurricane Camille, but Katrina topped every hurricane I've experienced. A week after my evacuation, evacuees were allowed back home for one day to gather their possessions before returning to their safe havens.

At the time, I lived in Metairie, Louisiana, near the notorious Seventeenth Street Canal. Fears galloped through my heart and mind. Was my house still intact? Did the massive floodwaters that breeched its levees carry my house away?

These worries and similar thoughts whirled inside me as I climbed into my car at my sister's house in Opelika, Alabama, my safe haven from this monster storm. I followed the highway westward across the state, into Mississippi and then southward. Every gas station I passed had empty pumps. As my gauge neared empty, I prayed hard till finally, I came upon a station whose pumps were still in service. I filled up my car; I continued into Louisiana.

As I neared home, since the interstate highways only allowed emergency vehicles and police traffic, state troopers detoured my car and others down back roads I never knew existed. I drove past swamps and into rural areas bearing no signs of life. Sheriffs' deputies and policemen directed our bumper-to-bumper traffic jams. At one point, all traffic stopped for too long a time. Would I make it home before the authorities enforced the curfew? I couldn't worry about that. It was out of my control, so I got out of my car to stretch my legs, only to climb back inside it due to a swamp's stench. At last, everyone's cars began moving at a crawl.

Once we got past the swamp and into a parish not hit as hard, traffic sped up. Alas, I reached my neighborhood before dark and before the curfew.

I gasped at Katrina's destruction. Trees snatched out of the earth by their roots, houses without roofs, stranded cars, boats cast up on medians whose hulls held holes resembling a torpedo strike. Oh, I'd seen such things before. Still, I struggled to take heart. Perhaps my house still stood.

I turned onto my street. It did! All the houses on my street were still standing! Despite damaged trees, roofs, and fences, they remained livable and unflooded.

Early that evening, while looking out my back window, I watched a lonely bird light on my fig tree. "That bird's meant for you," I heard God say. "I took care of him during the storm, and I'll take care of you."

Hurricanes will come, tornadoes will come, difficult times and various bad things affect us all. It's part of our human experience. But for those of us who know Christ, we can take hope as represented by the storm bird in my tree. During life's bleakest circumstances we always have hope. Hoping in God, indeed, is our blessing, our strength.

PRAYER: Thank You, Lord, for giving us hope in the midst of life's adversities. Thank You for being our strength and our shield, no matter what. In Christ's name. Amen.

Brief Reflection

How is hope a blessing?

Passages for Study

Psalm 16
Jeremiah 17:5-8
Titus 2:11-15

Study Notes

Bamboo

Philippians 4:15-20

But my God shall supply all your need according to His riches in glory by Christ Jesus (Philippians 4:19, *KJV*).

Seven days, seven miserable days and nights. Would it ever stop? The rain, I mean. At least I had an idea what Noah might have experienced. Hard, constant rain. Finally, the sun scattered the clouds and blue skies cheered my mood.

But for a moment. When I stepped into my back yard, I gazed through the woods behind my house. Trees were knocked down. So many in fact, that I could clearly see the red clay creek bank opposite my property a half mile away. My jaw dropped. *Oh, no! It can't have happened!*

I hurried inside my house and grabbed my binoculars. Back outdoors, I adjusted their lenses and got a closer look. Yep. The creek now resembled a lake, so wide it seemed to yawn at the sky. Sunrays filled huge gaps where dirt and foliage once stood. For all the years I'd lived here, it had always stayed narrow and usually dry, except when it rained.

I navigated a fast path between timbers and brush. Erosion. A chunk of river bank, succumbed to the incessant rain, lay far below. Also, the creek had changed course and now flowed against my property. If I didn't get a handle on it, it'd eventually reach my house atop a small hill. A mudslide would carry my house into oblivion as I'd seen in the movies. My imagination ran constant replays of it. Bricks strewn everywhere, banged up doors, shattered windows, house sliding and slipping down the slope. I worried.

Since the bank dropped some ten or twelve feet, a retaining wall was unaffordable. I came up with a solution. Ground cover and rocks.

I purchased rocks and bricks at a local hardware store and piled them into holes caused by uprooted trees. I also planted mongo grass, Asiatic jasmine, and English ivy for ground cover.

These ground covers may have worked fine, except they didn't grow fast enough. My checking account suffered from purchasing these things. My situation gave me no choice.

After every rain, I inspected the situation. My property continued to shrink. At a friend's suggestion, I finally called someone from the U.S. Forest Service and requested his help.

"There's not much you can do about it," he said when we went down to the creek. "It's just nature taking its course." Then he pointed out something I hadn't noticed—thin stalks of fast-growing bamboo. They'd started taking over this part of the creek. One of the best plants to stop erosion, I'd heard.

I don't know if the bamboo had been there before I moved into my house. Perhaps it was. But I rejoiced. God had taken care of me and loved me so much that He even took care of a landscaping issue.

As Paul told the Philippian believers, "… my God shall supply all your need according to His riches in glory by Christ Jesus." So instead of worrying and working to resolve issues on my own, like I had done, I simply had to put my problems in His hands, trust Him, and do whatever He led me to do rather than try to figure everything out. When we don't rely on Him we waste time, and in my case, also money.

PRAYER: Dear Lord, I place every situation I encounter into Your hands. Thank You for taking care of me and meeting my needs. In Jesus' mighty name. Amen.

Brief Reflection
Our God is faithful. Can we trust Him to meet all of our needs?

Passages for Study
Matthew 6:25-34

Study Notes

Buried Treasure

Proverbs 2:4-5

If thou seekest her as silver, and searchest for her as for hid treasures; Then shalt thou understand the fear of the LORD, and find the knowledge of God (Proverbs 2:4-5, KJV).

"Some pirates buried their treasure here." My great-uncle, seated at his kitchen table, eyed me over his cup of coffee.

"They did?" I plopped down on a sofa, my childish imagination pondering his statement.

"Somewhere around here. No one's found it yet." His serious tone and demeanor added a touch of truthfulness to his words.

A touch, yes, but...oh, I still questioned his words. I often accompanied my father on visits to his home in Pirate's Cove, part of the small coastal town of Josephine, Alabama. Every time I visited him, he repeated the same thing—pirates and buried treasure. Well...maybe...We were on the coast, weren't we? Was there a chance I could find it and become rich? Blackbeard's treasure? Captain Kidd's?

As I grew older, I realized his stories were merely that— tales told to entertain a child. Suppose it wasn't a mere story, though? Suppose what my great-uncle told me was true? To find it would've required a lot of effort using metal detectors, shovels, and similar things. I'd used metal detectors before, even found a buried metal garbage can once with them. I never bothered looking for pirate's booty, though. I had too much fun going out in his boat, fishing and occasionally scuba diving. Looking for something that didn't exist was a waste of time.

A real treasure "chest" sits inside our homes, in bookstores and libraries, and other places. What is it? Our Bible. Throughout the ages, men have tried to destroy it. It's been burned, banned, ridiculed. Yet, it still stands, blessing those of us who seek God's wisdom and guidance. We don't need metal detectors and shovels. We only need an insatiable hunger to dig into it and let the Almighty teach us.

PRAYER: Dear Lord, thank You for Your Word. Give me a hunger to learn more. Grant me a deep desire to seek You for direction. In Jesus' name. Amen.

Brief Reflection

Reading and studying our Bibles provides spiritual nourishment for Christians. If we fail to spend time in His Word, our spiritual lives will wither and die. What are some benefits of personal Bible study?

Passages for Study

Joshua 1:1-9
Psalm 119:105-112
2 Timothy 3:10-17

Study Notes

A Southern Boy's Final Word: *Where's My Trophy?*

I entered my sister's room and made a beeline to her trophies standing atop her chest of drawers, something I often did when she wasn't home. She was the athlete. I wasn't. Bummer! Why couldn't I be an athlete like her and my father?

My father played golf, my sister played tennis. At age 94, my father once shot an 81. I couldn't shoot a score like that even in college.

Regarding my sister, so it seemed to me, she collected tennis trophies as easily as picking up sticks.

I always counted her trophies, read the inscriptions on their brass plates...*Oh, if only I could win one, just one trophy to put in my bedroom.*

My insecurity and athletic ineptness steered me down a different path, the class clown's. I knew how to be funny, at least that was my opinion. Staying after school or getting sent to the office didn't curb my antics. I thrived on people's laughter, the bread and water that nourished my self-esteem. I was the family's comedian and prankster. That's all I cared about at the time.

In the sixth grade, my opportunity at "stardom" arrived. The Kiwanis Boys' Club[48] planned a talent show my father,

48 The Boys' Clubs are now called The Boys' and Girls' Clubs. This experience happened in the 1960s, before its name changed.

a member of its board, told me. Since I'd accompanied him to the Club on numerous occasions to play, I jumped at the chance. Settling on a stand-up routine similar to Bob Hope's, I memorized a few jokes I found in a joke book.

Alas, the day came. Showtime! Standing in the wings, I riveted my attention on the trophies lining the judges' table. Though nervous about telling jokes in front of a large audience, my burning desire for a trophy consumed my fears.

"Jack Cunningham!" the emcee announced.

I moved onto the stage, stood at the microphone, and told my first joke.

Silence responded. No. I did hear one sympathy laugh from a nice lady, her arms folded, who sat in the front row

I told my second joke.

One laugh from the nice lady in the front row. Her folded arms did not unfold.

All right. I'll get 'em with this one. I told the funniest joke I'd memorized.

From the nice lady. Front row seat. Arms folded. Laugh.

I descended the stage and re-entered the wings. From here I watched the comedy acts that followed mine. Laughter rocked the place. *Guess I lost another trophy,* I told myself, my spirits sinking.

The show ended. The judges started passing out trophies and congratulating the winners.

"In the comedy category." A judge leaned in close to the microphone. "Jack Cunningham."

Stunned, I went forward and received my award. On the way home, I pondered it. Turning to my father, I said, "I really don't deserve this."

"If you didn't deserve it, they never would've given it to you," he said.

Whether they gave it to me out of sympathy because I was a kid, or because I was the only comedy contestant who did a solo act, I'll never know. Deep down, I knew my performance stank. Yet still, I'd finally gotten that trophy I'd longed for. Soon as I got home, I put it up in my room.

Decades later, I have no inkling where that trophy is. It lost its meaning long ago.

Every gift, every talent we possess, comes from the Lord. His blessings come to us in many ways. The most important blessing is His eternal trophy, the "crown of life,"[49] which none of us deserve, just as I didn't deserve that talent show trophy. It's only by His grace through our faith that He's given it to those of us who trust Him.[50] Faith in Christ and His finished work on Calvary's cross.

AND THUS ENDS THIS
SOUTHERN BOY'S REFLECTIONS

---

49 James 1:12
50 Ephesians 2:8-9

Bibliography

Bishop, M.C. and Coulston, J.C.N. *Roman Military Equipment: From the Punic Wars to the Fall of Rome.* 2nd ed. Oxford, United Kingdom: Oxbow Books, 2006. Reprint 2009.

Boice, James Montgomery. *Ephesians, An Expositional Commentary.* Grand Rapids: Zondervan Publishing House, 1988.

Briscoe, D. Stuart. *Patterns for Power: Parables of Luke.* Glendale, California: Regal Books, 1979.

Broomall, Wick. "The Second Epistle to the Corinthians." *The Wycliffe Bible Commentary,* edited by Charles F. Pfeiffer and Everett F. Harrison. Chicago: The Moody Bible Institute, 1962.

Cole, R. Dennis. *Numbers.* Vol. 3B. The New American Commentary: An Exegetical and Theological Exposition of Holy Scripture, edited by E. Ray Clendenen. Nashville: B & H Publishing Group, 2000.

Gardner, Joseph L., editor, *Reader's Digest Atlas of the Bible: An Illustrated Guide to the Holy Land.* Pleasantville, New York and Montreal: The Reader's Digest Assocation, 1981.

Habershon, Ada R. *The Study of the Types.* 2 vols. New Enlarged Edition. Grand Rapids: Kregel Publications, 1981.

Lee, Philip. "Jordan River." *Holman Illustrated Bible Dictionary,* edited by Chad Brand, Charles Draper, Archie England. Nashville: Holman Reference, 2003.

McMillan, Malcolm C. *The Land Called Alabama.* Austin: Steck-Vaughn Company, 1968.

Vine, W.E. *Vine's Amplified Expository Dictionary of New Testament Words,* edited by Stephen Renn, Reference Edition. Iowa Falls, Iowa: World Wide Bible Publishers, Inc., 1991.

About the Author

John "Jack" M. Cunningham, Jr. is a graduate of the University of Alabama. He holds a B.A. in history and taught school in the New Orleans area.

He's been writing professionally for over thirty years. His work has appeared in numerous devotional and Sunday school publications, and Christian magazines. He's also been a contributor to B & H's men's devotional series, *Take Five*. His fiction has appeared in literary magazines. His two historical novels, a series titled Southern-Sons-Dixie Daughters, are published under the byline John M. Cunningham, Jr. They are available in e-book format at amazon.com. Paperback versions of these books are in the planning stages.

He's a speaker at writers' groups and a writing instructor. He teaches Sunday school at Frazer United Methodist Church in Montgomery, Alabama.

Visit his website at www.writerslighthouse.weebly.com.

Made in the USA
Columbia, SC
17 May 2018